Pip

By Sally Cowan

Tam

Pip

Pip, sit!

Pip sat.

Tam pats Pip.

CHECKING FOR MEANING

1. Who is Pip? *(Literal)*

2. What did Tam tell Pip to do? *(Literal)*

3. Why do you think Tam wanted to pat Pip? *(Inferential)*

EXTENDING VOCABULARY

sit	Look at the word *sit*. Can you think of other words that rhyme with *sit*?
sat	Look at the word *sat*. How many sounds are in the word?
pats	Look at the word *pats*. What is the base of this word? What has been added to the base? Can you think of another word that means the same as *pats*?

MOVING BEYOND THE TEXT

1. Why do you think Tam chose a rabbit for a pet?

2. Do you think a rabbit is a good pet? Why or why not?

3. What other animals can you train to do things such as sitting?

4. What are some different places that rabbits live?

SPEED SOUNDS

| Mm | Ss | Aa | Pp | Ii | Tt |

Tam

Pip

sit

sat

pats